# First World War
### and Army of Occupation
# War Diary
### France, Belgium and Germany

14 DIVISION
43 Infantry Brigade
King's Royal Rifle Corps
7th Battalion
2 February 1918 - 31 May 1918

WO95/1910/2

The Naval & Military Press Ltd
www.nmarchive.com
**Published in association with The National Archives**

Published by

# The Naval & Military Press Ltd

Unit 10 Ridgewood Industrial Park,

Uckfield, East Sussex,

TN22 5QE England

Tel: +44 (0) 1825 749494

www.naval-military-press.com

www.nmarchive.com

*This diary has been reprinted in facsimile from the original. Any imperfections are inevitably reproduced and the quality may fall short of modern type and cartographic standards.*

**© Crown Copyright**
**Images reproduced by permission of The National Archives, London, England, 2015.**

# Contents

| Document type | Place/Title | Date From | Date To |
|---|---|---|---|
| Heading | WO95/1910-2 14 Div-43 Inf Bde 7 KRRC Feb-May 1918 | | |
| Heading | 14th Division 43rd Infy Bde 7th Bn K.R.R.C. Feb-May 1918 | | |
| Heading | War Diary 7th K.R.R.C February 1918-May 1918 Vol 33 Volume 34. | | |
| Heading | 7th-(Service) Battalion The Kings Royal Rifle Corps. War Diary From 1st February To 28th February 1918 Volume 34 | | |
| War Diary | Clastres | 02/02/1918 | 02/02/1918 |
| War Diary | Ly Fontaine Trenches | 06/02/1918 | 18/02/1918 |
| War Diary | Clastres. | 26/02/1918 | 26/02/1918 |
| Miscellaneous | 7th. (S) Bn. Kings Royal Rifle Corps. | 28/02/1918 | 28/02/1918 |
| Heading | 43rd Brigade. 14th Division. 7th Battalion King's Royal Rifle Corps March 1918 | | |
| War Diary | | 01/03/1918 | 18/03/1918 |
| War Diary | Renay | 21/03/1918 | 21/03/1918 |
| War Diary | Jussy | 22/03/1918 | 23/03/1918 |
| War Diary | Faillouez | 23/03/1918 | 23/03/1918 |
| War Diary | Riez-Cugny | 23/03/1918 | 24/03/1918 |
| War Diary | Crasollas | 24/03/1918 | 24/03/1918 |
| War Diary | Beurains | 25/03/1918 | 25/03/1918 |
| War Diary | Porquericourt | 25/03/1918 | 25/03/1918 |
| War Diary | Thiescourt | 26/03/1918 | 26/03/1918 |
| War Diary | Elincourt | 27/03/1918 | 27/03/1918 |
| War Diary | Rieux | 28/03/1918 | 28/03/1918 |
| War Diary | Nogent | 29/03/1918 | 30/03/1918 |
| War Diary | Flagny | 31/03/1918 | 31/03/1918 |
| Heading | 43rd Inf. Bde. 14th Div. War Diary 7th Battn. The King's Royal Rifle Corps. April 1918 | | |
| Miscellaneous | Extract From The King's Royal Rifle Corps Chronicle. 7th Battalion War Records. | 31/03/1918 | 31/03/1918 |
| Heading | War Diary of The 7th (Service) Battalion The Kings Royal Rifle Corps Volume 36 From 1st April 1918 To 30th April 1918 Vol 35 | | |
| War Diary | Plachy | 01/04/1918 | 01/04/1918 |
| War Diary | Mourge | 02/04/1918 | 12/04/1918 |
| War Diary | Renty | 14/04/1918 | 14/04/1918 |
| War Diary | Aire | 15/04/1918 | 27/04/1918 |
| War Diary | Sains-Les-Fressin | 29/04/1918 | 29/04/1918 |
| Heading | Vol War Diary of the 7th (Service) Battalion King's Royal Rifle Corps. From 1st To 31st May 1918 Volume 37 | | |
| War Diary | Sains Lez Pressin. | 01/05/1918 | 01/05/1918 |
| War Diary | St Michel | 02/05/1918 | 02/05/1918 |
| War Diary | St Nicael | 06/05/1918 | 31/05/1918 |

WO95/1910-2

14 Div - 43 Inf Bde

2 KRRC

Feb - May 1918

14TH DIVISION
43RD INFY BDE

7TH BN K.R.R.C.
FEB-MAY 1918

From 41BDE 12 DIV

Returned to UK JUNE 1918
and Absorbed by
34 LONDON REGT

Vol 33

War Diary.

7th K.R.R.C

(February 1918 - May 1918)

Volume 34.

Secret.

17th (Service) Battalion

The King's Royal

Rifle Corps.

War Diary

From 1st February
To 28th February 1918.

Volume 34.

Army Form C. 2118

# 7th Bn. K.R. Rifles WAR DIARY for month of FEBRUARY 1918 VOLUME 34

## INTELLIGENCE SUMMARY
*(Erase heading not required.)*

Instructions regarding War Diaries and Intelligence Summaries are contained in F.S. Regs., Part II. and the Staff Manual respectively. Title Pages will be prepared in manuscript.

| Place | Date | Hour | Summary of Events and Information | Remarks and references to Appendices |
|---|---|---|---|---|
| CLASTRES | 2nd | | Bn. transferred to 43rd Infantry Brigade owing to a general reorganization. The Brigade was composed of the 6th Somerset Light Infantry and the 9th Scottish Rifles, the latter from the 9th Highland Division. The Brigade is commanded by Brigadier General R. TEMPEST, Scots Guards. | MJSA |
| LY FONTAINE Trenches | 6th | | Bn. moved to LY FONTAINE with 2 coys. and Transport at REMIGNY — On the 6th we relieved the 6th K.O.Y.L.I. in the front line at MOY. Dispositions — 2 coys. in front line, 1 in support, 1 in reserve. 6th S.L.I. on left alternating with 9th S.R., 58th Div on right. The front extended from J2D c to O1 c (sheet 66c) a distance of 3000 yards, and was mainly held by a series of detached posts with strong patrols out nightly. The ground in front of our line was very marshy, and the German line was somewhere near than 800 yards. The Bn. was in for 20 days with intermediary reliefs — The line was the quietest we had ever been in, though the enemy had the advantage of us in observation partly owing to little ground and partly because in his retreat he had felled every tree and levelled every building. We had our own batts in a tunnelled quarry just behind the front line, and the canteen in the same place did a great trade. | MJSA |
| | 18th | | On the night of the 18th/19th one of our posts was raided by the enemy. We lost one man who had only joined a few days before, as he was wearing brass buttons and was of very mean an intelligence we hope that he was incapable of giving any useful information. | MJSA |
| CLASTRES. | 26th | | On the night 26th/27th the Bn. was relieved by the 7th Royal West Kents 18th Div., and moved to CLASTRES at the tactical disposal of the 41st Inf. Bde. We spent 3 days the finding some working parties on rear lines in the intervals of "standing to" prepared to move at short notice. | MJSA |
| | | | Our total casualties during the tour were 5 O.R. wounded (3 self inflicted – showing the lack of training of recent drafts), 1 O.R. missing believed prisoner. Draft of 72 O.R. joined during the month. | |

J. Brown
Lieut Col
Cmdg 7th K.R. Rifles

## 7th.(s) Bn. Kings Royal Rifle Corps.

The average strength of Battalion during the month of February 1918 was :-

    35 Officers    935 Other Ranks.

    Of above

| Off. | O.R. | |
|---|---|---|
| 1 | 44 | were admitted to Field Ambulance |
|   | 25 | were evacuated out of the Divl. Area |
|   | 11 | rejoined from Field Ambulance |
| 1 | 8  | still remain in Field Ambulance. |

28/2/18.

                                    Lieut-Col.
                        Commd. 7th.(s) Bn. K.R.R.C.

43rd Brigade.
14th Division.
---------

7th BATTALION

KING'S ROYAL RIFLE CORPS

MARCH 1918

**Army Form C. 2118**

**WAR DIARY** of the 4*(Service) Bn*
*or*
**INTELLIGENCE SUMMARY**    K.R. Rif Corps

VOL: 35.

(Erase heading not required.)

| Place | Date | Hour | Summary of Events and Information | Remarks and references to Appendices |
|---|---|---|---|---|
| | 1.3.18 | | The Bn moved to REMIGNY in relief of the 9th Scottish Rifles, being then in Bde Reserve, where it remained for 12 days. On the 5th March a draft of 6 OR joined, and another draft of 6 OR on the 11th. | |
| | 9.3.18 | | Captain K. FRANCIS left the Bn. to do a 6 months tour of duty in England. | |
| | 12.3.18 | | The Bn relieved the 9th S.R. in the CERISY sector of the front line. The enemy's six days were notable only for extreme Liveliness. Active patrolling of No Man's Land was carried out nightly by dawn and the enemy's wire suggesting the resumption of his attempts to attack, and inviting him to surrender. A draft of 6 OR joined on the 15th. | |
| | 18.3.18 | | The Bn was relieved by the 6th Somerset Light Infantry, and proceeded into Bde Support with Hdqrs and 1 company at MONTESCOURT, and 3 companies in the neighbourhood of BENAY.

Lts. W.L. SANDERS, R.P. GRAHAM, and J.H. RODEN 2/Lt F.V. BAKER and H.M. DAY joined the Bn from the disbanded 21st K.R.R.C.
The position of Bde Reserve included in case of emergency the occupation of what was known as the "Battle Zone", a series of strong points in front of BENAY. As the Bn had not hitherto and forming the immediate defense of BENAY. However on the 20th it became known and occupied the area, it was divided 20/21st. However on the 20th it became known that this was fixed for the night 20/21st. However on the 20th it became known that 2 prisoners captured on the 19th, had stated that the great German offensive would start on the morning of the 21st. Consequently, though the test took place as pre-arranged, it was felt to be more in the nature of a precautionary measure than a test time and simple of the Bn. However, upon opening long cattle against any hostile activity. By midnight of the 20th/21st therefore, the Bn was in position in the Battle Zone with H.Q. and "A" Coy behind BENAY ("Bde Hqrs being in the same Spot), "C", "D", and B Coys occupying a series of strong points in front of BENAY from left to right, and A Coy in 3 more strong points in close support. The night was uneventful, | |

2149   Wt. W14957/M90 750,000 1/16 J.B.C. & A.  Forms/C.2118/12.

# WAR DIARY or INTELLIGENCE SUMMARY

Army Form C. 2118.

| Place | Date | Hour | Summary of Events and Information | Remarks and references to Appendices |
|---|---|---|---|---|
| BENAY | 21.3.18 | | and nothing could have been more peaceful. Everyone expected to remain in position till dawn and return then to BENAY. | |
| | | 3.30 am | The Colonel and Major R.A.W. LAYE returned to HQ after having been round the companies, and lay down for a few hours sleep. Major Dr. J. ELPHINSTON (2nd in command) had her left and the Transport at MONTESCOURT. | |
| | | 4.45 am | Everyone at Redoubts was awakened by the roar of a very heavy enemy barrage put on the front line. All communication between Bde and the front line Bn (6th Som. L.I.) was cut before any message from Bde could come through, and day broke with a visibility of less than 50 yards. Runners from the cap bright news of enemy shelling on the strong points; and although nothing definite was known of becoming of 2 companies of the 9th S.R. at REMIGNY were sent for, and a party of 50 OR. (Transport details from the 3 Bns in the Bde) from MONTESCOURT, under 2nd Lt T.G. GRAHAM of the Bn. Before long the shelling of the Battle Zone became heavier and more accurate, and the companies Bde and Br Hdqrs were subjected to a considerable bombardment. The enemy barrage lifted approximately two hours at the end of which the Bodies attacked. The advance of the Som. L.I. troops went to Bde HQ (about 11 am) were that his Br HQ and by the time he reached Bde HQ (about 11 am) the companies in the Battle Zone were already engaged. The left (C) and centre (D) and (A), after having been practically surrounded with the centre coy (D), after it was found that Capt. Hon. W. BORTHWICK had been killed, Capt CH. D. KING (B Coy) had been severely wounded and that Captain H. JACKMAN (A Coy) (both severely wounded and the that Captain Lt W.L. SANDERS (D Coy) succeeded in very skilfully (C Coy) and Lt W.L. SANDERS (D Coy) succeeded in very skilfully handle of the enemy, Capt C.H.D. KING (B Coy) succeeded in very skilfully withdrawing his coy, and a line was taken up along a sunken road running E and W about Gore Yole behind BENAY and on a level with BRANDON's hutts. This was reinforced by 2nd Lt BRANDON's party, he | |

# Army Form C. 2118.

## WAR DIARY or INTELLIGENCE SUMMARY.

*(Erase heading not required.)*

| Place | Date | Hour | Summary of Events and Information | Remarks and references to Appendices |
|---|---|---|---|---|
| | | | 2 supporting cos of the Scottish Rifles, and a few of the Bn. Reserve coy (mostly 2Lt J. McDONALD of the Bn.) held, and many enemy aeroplanes flew low during the afternoon. The fog lifted, and directing artillery fire on our lines firing M.G. and directing artillery fire. On the left of our line considerable numbers of Boches were seen advancing round the left of BENAY (and were successfully engaged with rifle fire). Bn. HQ had been moved back to their Battle position near the MONTESCOURT Railway Bridge. The line remained in this position until late afternoon, when it became apparent that the Boches were to our left rear, and a pistol gun was brought up to within 800 yds firing with open sights on Bn HQ rendering the position untenable. The left rear was thought to be about 250 yds into a wood there. Evidence of some establishment with the 42nd Bde on our left. HQ moved into a dug-out in Sunken road about 500 yds behind this line. During this period great exertion was done by 2 of our field guns firing shrapnel at 500 yds range from their position about 20 yds in front of our right (B Coy). About 6 pm Capt KING was mortally wounded, and shortly afterwards 2 Lt J. McDONALD also, both the remnants remained until midnight 21st-22nd, when orders were received to withdraw without any relief, to JUSSY, which were done. This position was maintained during the day 22 of OFFOY. The casualties already mentioned. 2 Lt VINCENT, RATHBONE, Jay, ALLEN were in addition to casualties already mentioned. Lt GRAHAM, 2Lts SHAW and JACKSON wounded and missing, and about had been killed. 2Lts SHAW and JACKSON wounded and missing. Remaining with Bn. Bn. were missing, killed wounded. Major PAYLANE, Captain PETERWYN-JONES(Adjt), 2/Lt OR JE BANGH, Major PAYLANE, Captain PETERWYN-JONES(Adjt), 2/Lt U-Lt VA. FAIR (A Coy) and 2/Lt T.G.GRAHAM, and 2/Lt F.V. ISAACSON (Signal Officer), total about 130 OR. |  |

# WAR DIARY or INTELLIGENCE SUMMARY

**Army Form C. 2118**

| Place | Date | Hour | Summary of Events and Information | Remarks and references to Appendices |
|---|---|---|---|---|
| JUSSY | 22nd | | After withdrawal from the "Battle Zone", the Bn proceeded to a position in rear of JUSSY, manning a spit-locked trench running horrizontally to and about 200 yds in front of the JUSSY – FLAVY LE MARTEL railway, and inclusive of the JUSSY – FLAVY and JUSSY – FAILLOUEL roads. Being in support to a front line established along the south bank of the JUSSY Canal, manned by the Sherwood Rifles and Border the 22nd was eventually established in a Cellar at the level crossing on the latter. H.Q. was above-mentioned roads. The 22nd was hunted in deploying this time. During the day, which was clear and sunny, the enemy reached the north bank of the Canal, and swept the whole of JUSSY, and the roads, continuously. The Canal, and fire. | |
| | 23rd | | During the night 22nd/23rd the enemy reinforced his attacks, and brought up M.G. fire. 22nd/23rd St Lancers, and 2nd Hussars – came up in support. Scots Greys, 5th Lancers, and 2nd Hussars – came up in support. cavalry. About 3 am a party of the enemy succeeded in forcing a crossing over one of the bridges which had not been blown up. Major M.J.G. AUBYN of the Bn, who had promptly assumed command of a mixed body of Brigade and Division of Details, immediately organised and successfully carried out a successful counter-attack, driving the enemy back over the canal, and restoring the situation. Major SPAUBYN was, however more unfortunately killed at the head of this very gallant and successful time accompanied by clouds of the 23rd dawn who for the third successive time. The situation on the at the situation became exceedingly obscure. Reports being received for our part became satisfactory, accentuated by a report of enemy being in broad flanks. It was never satisfactory, accentuated but the enemy had effected a crossing in force from the Division on our right, that the enemy was lent to the 29th of them at all costs, that Reinforcements would be sent to the 29th of Trench, where the enemy had T.C. CRAHAM and about 70 O.R. were lent in the morning the enemy 20 yards to the Right Front of Bn H.Q. later in the morning the enemy 6,000 yards to the Right and advanced on to our left. In conjunction with the S.R., the remainder of the Bn lived the Railway embankment to the left of Bn H.Q. and astride the JUSSY – FLAVY road, with The cavalry to the right of 2/HQ. The enemy | |

Army Form C. 2118.

# WAR DIARY
## or
## INTELLIGENCE SUMMARY.
(Erase heading not required.)

| Place | Date | Hour | Summary of Events and Information | Remarks and references to Appendices |
|---|---|---|---|---|
| Jisr | 23rd | | *[handwritten entry, largely illegible]* | |

Army Form C. 2118.

# WAR DIARY
## or
## INTELLIGENCE SUMMARY.
(Erase heading not required.)

| Place | Date | Hour | Summary of Events and Information | Remarks and references to Appendices |
|---|---|---|---|---|
| JUSY | 23rd | | [illegible handwritten entry] | |
| ENGLEFIEZ | 24th | 24h | [illegible handwritten entry] | |
| REZ-CHONY | 25th | 24h | [illegible handwritten entry] | |
| | | 2 P.M. | [illegible handwritten entry] | |

Instructions regarding War Diaries and Intelligence Summaries are contained in F. S. Regs., Part II. and the Staff Manual respectively. Title pages will be prepared in manuscript.

# WAR DIARY
*or*
# INTELLIGENCE SUMMARY.
*(Erase heading not required.)*

Army Form C. 2118.

| Place | Date | Hour | Summary of Events and Information | Remarks and references to Appendices |
|---|---|---|---|---|
| 25th CRISOLLES | 26th | | About 11 pm 26th orders were received to march to BEAURAINS, where the Brigade was posted in defence of the canal & bridge, with the S.R. in front and the Bn in reserve in billets in the village. (The canal was empty of water and could have been easily crossed at any point). | |
| BEURAINS | | | Here a number of [illegible] rejoined the Bn from leave, courses, etc. | |
| | 26th | | The following morning the Bn was ordered to move to a position on the ridge immediately in front of PORQUERICOURT, covering the main ROYE–NOYON road, HQ being established in the ~~—~~ Chateau de P. | |
| PORQUERICOURT | | | About dusk orders were received to march to a position S.W. of SUZOY, thence to THIESCOURT where the night was spent. | |
| THIESCOURT | | | On the morning of the 26th the Brigade moved into a wood about 1 kilometre west of THIESCOURT, where a halt was made and dinners eaten, the remainder of the Division being also in the vicinity. After dinners Bn marched to a [illegible] near ECOUVILLON, where the whole division rendezvoused, and Major RAWLINS rejoined and took command of the Bn, bringing with him a number of men of the Bn from Corps Reinforcements. | |
| | 26th | | In the evening the Bn moved to ELINCOURT for the night. | |
| ELINCOURT | 27th | | On the 27th the Bn marched to ESTREES SAINT DENIS, where Capt. G. RICHARDS (Q.M.) ~~and~~ Lt R.M. HUTTON (T.O.) and the Transport rejoined. | |
| RIEUX | 28th | | On the 28th the Bn marched to PONT-ST-MAXENCE, which was found to be full of French, so the march was continued the following [illegible] to RIEUX, which was also so full of French that half the Bn had to be billeted in the Church. | |
| NOGENT | 29th | | On the 29th the Bn marched to NOGENT, where a halt of 8 hours was made to wait for busses; ~~[illegible]~~ these, however, contrary to everyone's expectations, eventually arrived, and after an all night journey the Bn was disgorged at HERICOURT | |
| | 29/30th | | and [illegible] after breakfast continued the journey to PLACHY–BUYON | |

(A7092). Wt. W12839/M1293. 75 ,0.0. 1/17. D. D. & L., Ltd. Forms/C.2118/14.

# WAR DIARY
## INTELLIGENCE SUMMARY

| Place | Date | Hour | Summary of Events and Information | Remarks and references to Appendices |
|---|---|---|---|---|
| PUSCHY | 31st | | Bn still in pursuit of PUSCHY, and the days following the Bn was still under shell fire and subjected to occasional air machine gun and MG fire of the MK Enfer dugs B (like BN HQRS) occupied daily. Everyone went to sleep at the night of the 31st in trench about 4 Kilos [illegible] [illegible] [illegible] having formed to [illegible] a minimum in district since 24-27. | J Austin ? Col<br>Comdg 7th KRR |

43rd Inf.Bde.
14th Div.

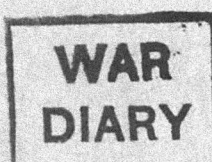

7th BATTN. THE KING'S ROYAL RIFLE CORPS.

A P R I L

1 9 1 8

## EXTRACT FROM THE KING'S ROYAL RIFLE CORPS CHRONICLE.

### 7th Battalion War Records.

1918
31st March.

The War Diary of this Battalion stops at this period, a matter of little consequence, as from the end of March the narative of the 7th Battalion as a Unit of the Regiment is of small interest.

On the 1st April, after receiving some scratch reinforcements, they moved by lorry to St. Nicholas in front of Amiens, and relieved a force of cavalry after dark in front of Domart. The next day they were relieved by the French, and falling back were in reserve to the 41st and 42nd Brigade until the morning of April 4th, when they moved up into support along the high ground 1000 yards South of Bois de Vere. The Germans did not attack the position. The next day Captain G.F. Jessup was severely wounded, and in addition our casualties were 6 killed, 23 wounded and 6 missing.

We were relieved from this part of the line on April 7th, and after much moving about reached Recklingham on April 14th, and the following day it was arranged we should form part of the composite Battalion with the 8th and 9th Battalions at Aire.

This arrangement, however, did not hold long, as on the 27th all except a nucleus of 10 officers and 52 N.C.Os and Riflemen, who were left to form a training staff for Americans, were sent to the Base as reinforcements.

The training Staff scheme was cancelled on June 14th and the Battalion Cadre was ordered Home, being transferred to the 16th Division, which they joined at Aldershot on 18th June. The Cadre was there formed the basis of a new Battalion, known as the 34th Battalion The London Regiment, and the 7th Battalion of the Regiment ceased to exist.

As the oldest Service Battalion they hold the honour of setting a fine example in patriotism at the first moment of their country's danger. How the High promise of their early training was fulfilled is set forth in the War Records of this Battalion published in the Regimental Chronicles of 1915 to the present volume, and requires no further comment. The Battalion fought with distinction through some of the hardest fighting of the War, and were finally overwhelmed.

---

Certified true extract.

Colonel.
Officer i/c Rifle Records.

Winchester.
30th October 1923.

Secret.

# War Diary

## of the

## 7th (Service) Battalion

## The King's Royal Rifle Corps

### Volume 36

From 1st April 1918
To 30th April 1918.

# WAR DIARY or INTELLIGENCE SUMMARY

Army Form C. 2118.

| Place | Date | Hour | Summary of Events and Information | Remarks and references to Appendices |
|---|---|---|---|---|
| PLACHY | April 1st | | The Bn moved soon after dawn by lorry to ST NICOLAS and spent the day there. Captain B.P. JESSUP, 2.L.I., late OC 43rd Bde T.M.Bty, joined the Bn for duty and assumed command of C Coy. | |
| HOURGE | 2nd | | On the night of the 1st/2nd the Bn moved up to relieve a force of Cavalry in front of DOMART and in front of HOURGE. After an eventful tour of 24 hours during which 7 OR were killed and 2 wounded the Bn was relieved by the French. Lt J.N. MARTIN was invalided to England. | |
| | 3rd | | Fifth being relieved the Bn proceeded to BLANGY WOOD where Lt Col the Honble E.T. HEWITT also Dorset Regiment returned and assumed command of the Bn. On the evening of the 3rd the Bn moved forward to billets in MAMETZ, being in reserve to the XVII Corps and 42nd Bdes in the line to the Bois de VAIRE. | |
| | 4th | | Early on the morning of the 4th the Bn turned out and moved up into supporting along the high ground about 1000 yds S. of the Bois de VAIRE. These trenches were dug in consequence and the 9th Seaforth Highrs and the GREYS L.I. The enemy somewhat repossession of the Bois de VAIRE but did not attack the position held by the Bn. The night of the 4/5th was passed in this position. | |
| | 5th | | On the morning of the 5th Lieut Capt G.E. JESSUP was severely wounded. The total casualties to OR in the three days' fighting 8 killed and 5 missing. | |
| | | | The Bn the Bn was relieved by the 2nd Australian Corps by a and CAVALRY and proceeded to billets in AUBIGNY. | |
| | 6th | | During the Bn marched back to dig a defensive position about 1000 y to the S of AUBIGNY. | |
| | 7th | | On the night of the 7/8th the Bn was relieved by Australians and marched to ST FUSCIEN to billet. | |
| | 8th | | 2/Lt C.R. HOGGE posted to Hd R.R.C. | |
| | 10th | | The Bn marched to SALEUX and arrived there by rail to CAMACHES thence by road to FERAUCOURT | |
| | 11th | | Following officers were sent to join the 2/4 R Division: Captn G.R. SUTCLIFFE, 2/Lts S.W & 2nd Lt J.W. MOORHOUSE (K.O. L.I. attd), 2/Lt L.J. HEATON (West Yorks. attd), 2/Lt S.R. COTTRELL, G.A. LAWSON, J. KETCHELL, and W.A. KNIGHT D.C.M. and 2/Lt B.S. The Bn marched to EnLearn at EU, and moved by road to HESDIN, thence thence thence | |
| | 12th | | to RENTY. | |

# WAR DIARY
## or
## INTELLIGENCE SUMMARY.

*(Erase heading not required.)*

Army Form C. 2118.

Instructions regarding War Diaries and Intelligence Summaries are contained in F. S. Regs., Part II. and the Staff Manual respectively. Title pages will be prepared in manuscript.

| Place | Date | Hour | Summary of Events and Information | Remarks and references to Appendices |
|---|---|---|---|---|
| KEMMY | April 14th | | The Bn. marched to RECLING-HEM. On the following morning 9 officers and 575 O.R. were sent to a form at employers Battalion with The 8th and 9th Regts. at AIRE. Details | |
| AIRE | 15th | | and Transport moved back via LAIRES to WAMBERCOURT | |
| | 27th | | On the 27th The Bn was distributed, 3 officers (Major RAM CAVES, 2nd Lt S. CLARKE and F EVANS) and 485 O.R. being sent to the 8th as reinforcements and a inclusive of 10 officers and 53 N.C.O.S and R/R being left to form a Training Bn for Americans | |
| SAINS-LES-FRESSIN | | | The Training Staff moved to SAINS-LES-FRESSIN. | |

C.J.Hans Lt Col
Cmdg 7 KRRC
1.5.18

# War Diary

of the

7th (Service) Battalion,

King's Royal Rifle Corps.

From 1st to 31st May 1918.

Volume 37

Army Form C. 2118.

# WAR DIARY of 7th Bn. K.R.R.f.C.

## INTELLIGENCE SUMMARY.
(Erase heading not required.)

VOLUME 37.

MAY 1918.

| Place | Date | Hour | Summary of Events and Information | Remarks and references to Appendices |
|---|---|---|---|---|
| SAINS LEZ FRESSIN | 1st | | The Battalion Training Staff were still at SAINS LEZ FRESSIN | Rh. |
| ST MICHEL | 2nd | | Four Company Commanders & N.Os. & N.C.Os. proceeded on Courses at the 1st Army School. The remainder of the training staff moved to ST. MICHEL. | Rh. |
| ST MICHEL | 6th | | Capt. Llewelyn Davies M.C. left to join the British Mission attached to X th French Army | Rh. |
| | 7th | | Officers & some of the N.C.Os returned from 1st Army Schools. 2/Lt. PRSMITH N.C. assumed duties of acting Adjutant vice Capt Bowin M.C. | Rh. |
| | 9th | | Lt. A.H. Bond M.C. (Somerset Light Infantry) posted to the Battalion | Rh. |
| | 12th | | Major F.B. WILSON (K.O.Y.L.I) joined the Battalion. L. HTTON & Transport left for C.U.C.O. | Rh. |
| | 13th | | Lt. Col. Hon. E.J. HEWITT, D.S.O. (DORSET) left for ENGLAND & Major E.B. WILSON took over Command. | Rh. |
| | 13/27th | | During this period training was carried out consisting of musketry, lectures & recreation, tactical schemes and also range practices on the range at OURKLEY. | Rh. |
| | 22nd | | The Battalion Training Staff moved to SAINS LEZ FRESSIN. 24th 2/Lt. V.A. FAIR left to R.A.F. | Rh. |
| | 25th | | The Divisional Commander visited the Battalion. Capt. K. Stainer rejoined Battalion. | Rh. |
| | 26/31st | | Training in the vicinity of SAINS LEZ FRESSIN was carried out during this period. H/S. Cook rejoined Battalion on 28/5/18. | Rh. |

E.B.Wilson Major
Commanding 7th (Service) Battalion
King's Royal Rifle Corps.